Disturbances of Progress

Disturbances of Progress

Lise Downe

Coach House Books

first edition

Published with the assistance of the Canada Council for the Arts and
the Ontario Arts Council

NATIONAL LIBRARY OF CANADA CATALOGUING IN PUBLICATION DATA

Downe, Lise
    Disturbances of progress / Lise Downe. – 1st ed.

ISBN 1-55245-112-7

    I. Title.

PS8557.O829D47 2002   C811'.54   C2002-904657-2
PR9199.3.D587D47 2002

for Fred and Tristan

From this wrought sense we do escape.

Contents

As If

It was with from which
who lost no grace
and spilled not so
by all that in.

While each in each
would see at last
some accord flung forth.
(What we of course.)

Why say not so
this just and sundry.
You bet sustains
through all and all.

As to these matters
and thus thus far.

Why procure.
Why firm.
You you
and such.

The Shadow of Your Simile

I ran out of you
having raised the question.
Now knowing what to believe in.
Travel broadening everything
even in absence.

Like cathedrals   from time to time
lengthening the days so that ultimately
there is no difference between
a little bit
and this welcome expanse which

makes you seem smaller.
Small enough to fathom that
still life.

Someone
(maybe me)
imagining the flowers arranged with contrasting shadows.
No one single image
only this unprecedented polyhedron
hand-painted   light tumbling
like light.

Long enough for the amaryllis to bloom.
Globe-trotting   like luggage
to greet the room.

With Rumi

If anyone asks to hold the essence
of a fine and foreign hand.
How measures of eloquence satisfy
all of our

Or how a small cord coiled will look
where crimped and say
    a series of circular lines
    like this.

When someone mentions
the abundance of a night sky.
Fabulous alignments climbing
what must have been
the roof.

Corresponding
        as all things do to us
once touching   the uncovered moon
your robe correspondingly
wants to know what 'spirit' is.

Will kiss the smaller rings and point.
Fingers visible and tipped.

This Then

I want to say that today is Friday.
That in a year of shortened hair
pleasures remind the indefinite day
that it too will come.

And then this welcome urgency unfolds
behind the letter 'E'.

I want to you know the taste of something much finer.
The importance of this clock growing older.
How a whistle blows as it draws from its envelope
    vellum
itching to be Wednesday instead.

I hope that a handful of folded papers will touch
this generous impulse and
   – it's frustrating but –
a bright idea though blind is better than nothing.

And then

    the voice

           yes

                falters
    wistful

after what seemed like eons
kindling the air with a searching glance.

    'Wow!'

and *now* look who's boss.

Their Profiles

Into summer's hidden cove
for the sake of an elsewhere
or a single limb's promise in the midst of
some tangible
   'Any further orders sir?'
man with a fish to fry.

I
   'That will be all.'
was installed intuitively
not in
but in all things to play
by ponytail to log it
until our timber shall policy.

Why then plan a marriage?
or the purchase of transport
of cardigans or comfort
in whom such rich simplicity
your windshield
and we by George speak ultimately
of that long night's journey.

Address the tender target head on.
Great sighs of relief amid
the uninhibited *and* dramatic.

Split Charity

What more could there be
extending 'Yes, but ...' to certain reproach
to conserve and happily increase
multiple points of usage.

What pursues ontological and explicit
reference, such as 'Find him!'

More in a given place
at lengths to what we speak of
as volumes thread
many a clustered or rotary dial.

Partly to what is purpose
a noble stretch unbuttons
them a watch and tracing
what have you.

Which is exactly the junction of traditional
lines that attend an elevated terrace
once seen as tomorrow
now up for
(and this defies time)
the night.

Credibility.
The royal standard now rarely
allowing for all that rapture.

'But, yes ...' for this marvellous breakfast
a slow
          (but gratifying)
                    climb.

But Oh To Ride Her Marvellous Exception

Many hours crave a slender paddle
flocking distinctions on either side of
a glass plane.
We ourselves a friction that emulates
the distance between days.

To stretch equatorial this long age.
Tide pool.
Neat oval of stones.

Through no-man's land
(by all accounts ailing)
I'm afraid   I'm afar   not one
who interiors but
unwavering.

So harpooned and only now surmised as what
not what or whom.

Synchronous digging thrills a personal fortune
at the boundary where Alice is hastening.
Not   on some tropical island
but while muttering into darkness
        dear   dear.
Must we apologize for my appearance when straddling
the swift horse?
Smell of orange pungent and constant
built up (the tiny miniatures)
to be little more than a whim
a whiff
and sneeze by first light.

★

Teased by thoughts that reservoir an iridescent surface
hypothetical meteors propel that single blonde.

So there she flies giddy.

Through an undulant haze
cocoa   rococo
tintin and rin tin tin
come to resemble each other.

Rising and falling all part and parcel
of what's here
or almost.
An utterance for instance
no longer horizontal.
Unfurling.
                    An outcry.
                              So so.

                    So then.

What To Believe

Inasmuch as striving is in exact proportion
to a dusted hat at nightfall.
And a gangplank to verify what served what quarter
of a century not without.

That a dollar and a half at ten thousand feet
could afford to not purchase
on principle.
That 'Well, well, well' should have it
in order to echo.

Of course 'Eh, what?' doesn't serve much purpose
save to trigger a halo or old apprentice
while they, succumbing
to some handsome return
at present, won't last forever.

One line unravels the article in question.
A gangplank waits to be given
        the word 'Go!'
in addition to a harebrained plus nebulous interest
that equals a critical eye.

Vignette

Even these magnificent doorknobs
metamorphose into figures
around a table of nibbling.
(the table periodically)

A cushion and cracked windowpane
so many stringed instruments
play some still life
before turning.
(the volume unheard of)

As though your feet
thus tortoise
could induce our tempted sighs.

The differed tone stumbles.
The cuff a pair and lately
urge only
(their whispers when)

from the still and essential
these twelve winds animate
figments of fragmentation
triggered by recent rain.

High drama on the low seas parallel
(under duress)
her dress gondola lacework
and a clutch of arms
ever so slightly wed with dew.

Necessary Surface

It was said she carried on
had wagered a cold winter with open hair
attendant and at times summoning a careless visitor
(unlike ourselves).

It seemed important to question
not only the right and elder.
Important because mountains had been inclined
and a little resentful
of those that fell in   then out
of focus.

Some had wanted to laugh
say it all goes in one ear and out.
The other not wanting to visualize *too* clearly.
Lest she.

Falling into place had had
to rest and cancel on special occasions
their influence.
My goodness their charm and cleverness.

Habit chancing those slim days
playing the company off by heart
then forgetting what it was for hours
– really grammatically –
as if to say, 'Not really listening'.
Presuming one ought to have an accent
or *some*thing.

(Some ecstatic impulse that leaps in spite
of them there there my child.)

My lessons.   My friends.
My morsels.

I should simply decline the steps too easily.

Foreheads imply eventual
and time (so that was it!)
is passing.

Remember to jump up
instructing guesswork in all your studies
with do   and and
and during.

Advances

As far as we can tell a foothold
by its size and means
unsettling ease in moods or the interval
between branch or tree.

Whether by willow or chance
it dares not stray from inference
overlapping like shingles
concentrations called towns.

The basis of a wall is where resemblance ends
effecting insular while standing
and so to shape it.

And so distinguishing the unsettled day
the consistency of appearance epitomized
deftly
admitting locomotion into this still state.

The whole ceiling shines
elusively hooting.

Labyrinthine recesses yield the consequence of
inattention in exaggerated hours
while a near-identical foothold remains
by and large and therefore
a ratio of its size that means
unsettling.

This the new ubiquity
bright mist of a night-flying flock
anxious to define 'smallish'
– even say a speck –
flat and posturing brief before you.

Imagine this group
its magnitude and friction and how
this applies to sediment.
Particle
by particle.

Try to maintain clarity.
Sounds simple enough
(but concentrate).
A tall   totemic   figure.

A leaf.   A toil.
Wherewith a two.
The question of how driven
driven by some nagging doubt.

The swift the swiftest
the and the 'twas
strange 'passing strange'
just browsing briefly.

This quality of echo wherewithal
last vestiges in tandem
(nonetheless)
still creep at the end of an allotted span.

Sweetheart of Commotion

A day like today in a wordless way
could well lead to speculation
for thatching the crowded and coastal
of our less fortunate sister.

A day of stained glass and spellbound
washed and graduated
the way without knowing
a cruel tenderness.

When   in presence of mind
a change introduces itself
with elegance and frequently impractical demands
to simply visualize the indefinite moment
(not one we'd grown accustomed to)
provides a graceful bow
uncurling and membrane.

The impasse of no shoes and a battered hat
shatters with fearful efficiency
the lack of proportion
lack of precision
given design.

Dual natures identify lunatic and
worthy companion with equal alacrity.
No advance notice.

Thereby central to any star-shaped configuration
responding one section at a time
to the by-no-means-formal procession ricocheting
with magnificent coordination.

'Disturbances of Progress' located where inspiration hovers
inhaling such thrill for evidence
eyes akimbo
of just how strong the passion is

worth holding onto.

Repercussions

Outside the flashlight's beam
yet inseparable from it, it is
as though the shining tool made visible
an inkling

insisting that gossamer thread
its really elementary and wholly unexpected overture
remain unceasingly active

untangling, rewinding
(by the rarest of happy chances)
the prospect of afterimage reminiscent of firefly.
Dots and spaces a magic of strings
unarrangeable
like the nature of sometimes.

Then doubling back
circumnavigating means and end
to track and root the trumpet and spiral
primordial in us as well as
in

creasing the odds of eclipsing the almost
certainly sound but more to the point
finding an equal footing that might establish
an idea of absence on par with the best of them
but *this* time with a whirling tail.

Border Crossing

How gracefully this door fulfills its orders
deliberately opening and closing and
opening the house built from spoils
in which the fox so strikingly figures.

A fortress. A raft. A tackle.
A network of cables.
From within the miniseries and terrors
provide a starting point for flights of starlings
no less startling than the eventual, inevitable
miseries and errors. To us a far cry.

From afar, the watchful eye of the king of attics
spills enough ink to flow haphazard
past an arrangement of stilts
posted once and presently as sentries.

How, then, such affinities unwittingly surpass
all lines of reasoning, running aground on the shoals
of an obsolete olfactory apparatus.
Its olfactory markings emit true vowels
such as 'oo' and 'ah'.
And 'ah'.

The decoy
(incapable of distinguishing nuts from grapes)
inhabits the splendour of its bindings
darkening the rule prescribed
beneath a makeshift plastic cover.

This the accepted state of affairs, its
dimensionality and weirdness improbable
yet entirely convincing. A cartoon.
And bulging.
Inside. Outside.
Boat. Swim. Bugle.

More widespread than anyone
would have believed.
I know *I'm* relieved.
Overwhelmed even, like the lepidopterist
for whom the 'plop' of a fish hitting the water
proves now and forever unbearable. From time to time
he'll tap on an improvised wooden stool
mesmerized by the visage of a fallen stump
where once had stood a standing tree.

His absence develops a mind
to deliberately ignore the plastic
and add something to an unregistered letter.
Its sixty-odd words have the strangest effect.
The smaller the number of syllables, the greater
one's need. Ridiculous and quaint, perhaps
to the unfed masses, but

Without henceforth beating one's wings within
some old, cold oven, let's cast our gaze
beyond these overly expectant woods.
Sensationalize our hair with royal jelly.

And the ornaments?

We'll apply them to the weapon as well as the wound.
We'll repent (apparently)
but not too soon.
First, we'll say goodbye to the dogs. The kittens.
Then the faunal reservoir.
Lasting recollection of them.

I'm trying to decide if one ought to fold
or appeal to more forgiving chapters.

Here lies the line of reasoning.
The gulf that separates
them by the store and starving

from us by the stove and staring.
Basking in the light of what we know
or thought we knew.

Well-fed. But lonely.

Volumes

By far is somewhat flexible
expanding apertures replete but in
the distance a past informed by hazard
and how to respond to them.

We could ask does it
or did it apply structural effectiveness
the rules by which.

What limits and under what do they?
What happens to the single?
What bears the course charting it?

How much finds itself when the meaning of house
is in short or any part thereof?
Of course inferring the much less frequent
from optimism.

Here a population lives.

Sometimes an absolute term
is forecast, is therefore
mobile suspending latitude with only
the slightest suggestion.

Tentative rests rarely
what with those so-called so strong and all.
Its members interlaced to a growing edge

which is open.

The cavity tempting.
One factor observed encircling
and sometimes a home is very large.

What is certain seems like plenty.

High tides of the wettest kind determine
unexplained fits of salt spraying.
Hazardous theory in visible flashes
signals both high and dry.

Nautical imagery may be momentary.
But extracts in that ocean lay bare
– as a wave does –

quivering and sundry

a path to a place
where green reception and pale yellow glow
recall a warmth you can't put your finger on.
(The precarious flame lit literally.)

And where not wearing socks augments the pleasure
of a surface we all can stand up in.

Rarity Escapes

Not being a child but being.
Sprightly although descending the not-yet
still scarce.
Yellow still gingerly across the tall
and rickety.
Town and stars.

A thoroughfare of striped partitions
attract now
the stormy compound open to the not-yet lit.

No litany of off less likely
to settle for some dimly inscribed
is it   ornament?
YES above a month of tides
and travelling.
Necessity of *this*.

Hence the curtain's flirtations compel by degrees
by declaring henceforth and sometimes
the mystery of an untidy room
speaks for and of.

For anything in a warm cloak shall humour
the house with no doors:
        tenuous groupings of structural detail
        ornate insets
        no slamming.

Didn't we speak of necessity with regret
by means and justly?
Not from forgetfulness
but for whom flowed from.
Becoming more comprehensible like 'hard' and 'currency'
with little or no hope of

And yet they participate
those circles of light.
Their fledgling ways a kind of surprised affection.
Others on the other lost hand

Can we blame them
those images of clay?
As if difference inferred a fact of single elements.
Plucked early they mingle.
Buoyant
the other car bare.

Vistas of distant parts
stars

But mobility, flesh and imagination astonish us
engender carnival and sparkles
inside and out this oh-so-decibel
oh-so-fluttering
every so hour
day after day
for the sake of the colony.

As for thin air
well

These Far-off Days

When light accompanies elsewhere
steady blackout and reverence
go with them
like an influx.

An alternate arrangement utters a single word
such as 'throng'.
And what to reply when reply seems strange to you?
What say the visitor?

Curtains hang as if almost.
The open palm
the lamp
the lot of them instead of lines.
Paper streamers a plethora.

And would once asserted
cause a lustre a rustling.
So, too, the latter half on a figured ground.

The composite look of which we spoke.
Odd.
Illustrative even.
Flared and tapered sleeves ushering
until all the profiled edges are shining.

Succession

In mid-air blessings defy gravity
are described as are likely to be
a shoe or sandal as they stand
save for an error of judgement.

There is a recognized place to which
we will give
            at a future date
our fuller consideration.

A double of the sentence is offered.
Here.   Here.

Introduction as conscience
foreshadowing a more complex past.
It gathers.

The contrary reversed.
It figures.

Nothing new in melancholy as
it dost wreak havoc with unleashed sentiment.

It could never be a noun.

Increasingly we are going to conclude
that clay presupposes the 'dust-to-dust' thesis.
In a pinch it is safe to assume.

A shudder now a conference
intent on shedding an enormous burden.

No telling the taking away.
Nothing in its wake.

For those who lower their voices around fragile objects
we offer this auditory association.
Some ill-tuned instrument punctuates the peripheral domain.

It does them good.

(As it were.)

We choose the sandglass to replace
an estimate with something symmetrical.

And hence.
And hence.

All these time zones.
Everyone present.

In olden days roses used to stink.
This   not the flowers   but the word.

'Humorous' shows a highly developed imagination
and fine spacing.

Other words on the other hand.
Prevalence of proportion.

In what direction does *your* hand soar upward?

Flashes of red   green   blue.

Fugitive revelations by way of illustration.

A radio was never a church.

Threshold

like ambrosia

like August

pardon me, Miss

this verse personifies

which is driftwood

the motto the

drums or halos

There's one!

laughing loudly

inflected, notably

just so and this

your sins?

intuition and diplomacy

smoothly, naturally

this thistle lectures

and why when

unchaperoned

as though consistent

so hard to grasp

or illumined

successive pairs

daylight hovers

Who really knows?

it into

even then

between one and ten

in pulses

it moot

the vivid colours this

by claiming

walls of which

a country

can still hear her

nothing quite like

apparently errant

flawless, lawless

more real

sometimes campy

more potent charms

What?

as well as well

let alone

remedy and try

fringing

of a no-win

pressing need

perhaps you've heard

siphon

Dare I say 'hark'?

percussion, string and wind

that is

accounts flicker

allegro allegro

hear and know

the routine will fail

word and image

the routine will fail

momentary and

the bridge

what a surprise to

esoterica

in the face of

the bridge

whatever square defines

town

through eyes of another

town

Novella
(a sort of harmony in which three characters)

Expedition

where and when
most ascents mostly
as scenery, and scenery

Immensely Cobbled, Unique Perhaps

farther afield and smaller
first, faster and most
pasture the notion

The Miracle and The Place

double take and the interim
by and by
there there is

is is
to imagine

41

Equals

Each and every acquaint themselves.
The mysterious tribe.
Convoluted scenario.

In places a small map imitates
the press and caress of an otherwise
obscure spot.
Evenness of its surface.

Everything with otherwise from which to choose.
A table in a field of rain
in a field after the rain.

The morning after
the disproportionate dream implies
a certain logic.

Each in every increment
initiates a drop of liquid
slightly displaced.

Silhouette of an airborne armchair.
The onset of shade coinciding with
with the arrival of clouds.

For, in passing

Each and every acquaint themselves.
Infectious laughter.
Its agents and apostles.

Unified by their reference and spatial link
the variant provides an otherwise
misplaced modifier
most salient and timely.

Everything so happens in the open air.
Aerial view.
Clouds escaping

into the bright blue present
the presence of magenta cones
confounds the bluest of days.

Every cone tip suspends
a single drop of liquid.
Like belief

the epic of how coincides
accordingly
with neither the sky in question

nor the shepherd, yonder.

*

Each and every acquaint themselves.
The mystery of this.
An issue of seasons.

What this might mean
might willingly forgo
an otherwise sullen
or sudden epiphany.

Every step taken proceeds accordingly.
What is Heather's name?
What in heaven's name

remains a reservoir
or singular blueprint
ever so slightly displaced.

Each and every fabulist
in so doing
ripples a peculiar logic.

We be will we
beside a stone pool giggling.
The way we will be

thus, in the morning.

Each and every reacquaint themselves.
What steps to be taken.
The guise a hollow.

A chain of former obsessions
heightens the contrast
between swollen and stolen.
Wouldn't have it otherwise.

Wouldn't this thus marvel
neither more nor less
or follow inflection's inflow and outflow.

Now full. Now empty.
Its links beget
a semblance of eddies and windows.

Each ringlike pattern
a lingering theft
with which we conspire accordingly.

Some troubling surge.
The sky a swell
to which the water adheres.

Unsettling, as nebulous as

Part Character, Part Study

If, in infancy
one finds oneself
considering the facts of marble, rushes
and flukes
one might unwittingly stumble upon
the making of tools to make the tools
that flip, turn and slide

whistling into the Renaissance
of late afternoon, for instance
and whirling there step out to see
where one has arrived
if one has arrived

breathless, in fact
before the crayon enlargement
waiting for what rises from the tapered river
and enters the sky-blue sky.
All, in short
without flinching.

Opportunity Knocks

No single irregularity prepared us.
Simply the street, its men of letters bestowing
convivial and constant attention upon the most
bewildered of two substances.
Where choice might fall, scarcely rounded
or surrounded.

Telegrams from the interior materialize without warning.
Where beck might call.
Cannot. Canto.
Mathematicians of our tongue well tell an easy alliance.
Of variations of.
That stretches just in case.

The Overseer

Out of sight and sound come casting spells
on tiptoe, advancing always. Tell me
what certainties of the near and distant
assemble before us? Don't they require
a certain amount of time to unpack?

Let's confide a certain thickness to every occasion
with the exception of those few porcelain hurdles.
Their invariable sighs rise and coalesce.
Affinity looms large, obliterating parts of

the scaffolding. Up, up, up.
The thinner side of a beam left far behind
venturing through a field of openings.

A filtering as lookout lends definition.
Not shadows, but glimmers.

One hand on the lintel

                                   farther, too far

for eavesdropping, yet resonant sensations jostle to strike
just the right chord. Hymns multiply

the piece, the passage, the dialogue between.
So that we convince ourselves afterwards, further on
every gesture (no matter how rich

or perverse) was something of a surprise.
All fine phrases retreat from the realm we are in
to something of a whisper.
Uh-huh. Uh-huh.

Consider the film. The narrow workroom long since blurred.
Rely on a certain softness to destabilize
the heavy apparatus. Try to convey, briefly
(hence only perilously) a sense of the platform
where a chair stands folded.

Only Wonder

In what direction do we find the formula for the salve? A place
for portraits? Kindness? A doctrine of signatures?
What is free rein in the still unnamed?
What is bridge?

What do we understand as temporary when all points
point towards an eternity now rapidly receding?
What are the chances we'll still be around to witness them
so far off the beaten path?

What difference rain or shine?

What is delinquent?
What is sacerdotal and how do we know what to give up?
What characterizes silence?

What is possible but seems truly unlikely?

What is 'masterful rural'? Or 'seldom reaches'?
What *really* happens under water?
What twigs the heron?

What is nocturnal in habit, thin and crenulate?
Of the three that are cited, which attracts?
And what of this 'fictitious bait'?

What carries the linguistic equivalent of a short fork
albeit grudgingly?

Whose cast?
Whose characters?

What lies under the impression? Alongside
or even above us?
What exalts?

Consolation

If only commodious
were the only issue.
If
not just by your utterance
but back a bit.
The steps swallowed whole
left uninhabited.
Wide-eyed and wondering

If the consequence of weird feet
were then juxtaposed
by a hyphen
grounded on the premise
that undulates in spite of
in spite of.
Shock infusing everything.
Everywhere.

One of whom and one of whom
one then may gather.
To turn, then
these anomalies, their pockets
useless unless the two overlap
like a fortune cookie.
Luckily.

Before and After

At the time of
the alleged
innovation
there had been talk
staggering
takes on
the issue
of
impropriety.
Of technique.

A hint about how
and
with one master stroke
Alice and I share the luxury
of the same
forbidden zone.

Up 'til now
comets replaced rumours.
'Twas foolish not to know it
reading left for right
for the inside line
until
it described a complete circle.

All those
details made them puzzling.
One ought to have

And then
there followed that
infamous night when
nothing happened.

Remnants
grafted onto the side of
that tree
at eye level
without the glasses.

All that was familiar yielded
unlikely thrills in an open grove.
An ideal indeterminancy.

Parameters changed the ones
who set out
leaving us free to think everything
smoothly tiled, as if
disposition and fingering were
tangible histories.

A new way of asking.

Remember that night?
Its gentle mania.
Suspended flight.

It came up centuries ago, abbreviated
and redirected the light.

Even so, oval windows remain too cautious
to entertain the notion of sound from shape.
Or whispering cloisters.

They, they've been there
open like that, for a long time.

One can scarcely count the multitude of rags
woven against them. They look duller now
less vivid. Sort of in a state of melt.

I've been told their reef is real
but the fish aren't.
What do you think?

Do you find me changed?

You hesitated, consulting the moment
then said:

>It was in you all along
>in the depths of your trembling hands.
>Pray meditate upon its poetry.

Such Ministrations None Dare Say

No more the compact image aimed at the belated.
No more false coins.
No more catastrophes bolstered through divine intervention.
No more cursory inspections of ladders poised
on ledges of sudden tumult, moulded
to rhythms of nervous lethargy.

Even when weary, remember
the kitchen tap by scallop and alabaster.
Applaud the infuriated with singular animation, stratagem
and guile. Awaken from doldrums and shallow depressions
for all fluctuations try to disguise
– and siphon –
nuance even in thought.

Prolong the waiting.
Hearken back to inhabit the disturbed question:
    How do I know?
Its girds. It loins. Its thousand hesitations radiate
ambiguity at different rates.
The more. The moor.

Terrain where downhill connotes not downfall
(the barber's interpretation)
but omnipresent flowers described in a triangle
– three times –
underlining all that is otherwise so hard to grasp
like geometry that lingers in an empty room.

This was the strategy.
To speculate on the terminology of location.
Locals orient themselves.
Rain is pouring.
Its habit unshaken.

Mince in Time

What 'in the end' means
in this world and the next

dwindles the sermon it speaks
through, rather than delivery

managing to sound
so dedicated.

While elsewhere
mingling errant among the epiphanies

and vast hydraulic systems
lockstep signifies that nowadays

off-hours are oft-times best described
as dried-up little things

a bunch of everlasting

and *lots* of musty.

Premonition

A handful implies a brilliant future
for which we posit surges.
Hygienic measure, forbidden zones
one cannot speak for

All one can do is challenge then
the antechamber's cry
as though a multitude were trying
to hide

The centre referred to could be this building
had had on guard the night
entwined

        'Look up. Wa-a-a-y up.
        And I'll call Rusty.'

I thought

        'Thus far I'm

Angle of Approach

Hard to estimate the depths to which
a cluster of verses might sink, superimposing
novelty and action on what appear to be
clouds of dust on a once-distinct horizon.

A cupful of water. A nest of bubbles.
Endless explanations milling around, tethered
to a single oyster that may
or may not be real.

Froth spun out under a banner that reads:
    Day in.   Day out.
And perhaps on occasion harbouring its own bent
beholden to the art of crest and trough.
Now loath to forgo.

From the right perspective the flag's embellishments are legion.
One couldn't say the same for the hang of things
tacked on for good measure.
Or the observatory at Paris.
Its inertial reference spilling out loud and clear.

Which carries us back, always to awaken
the overripe dates now whitened with chalk.
From afar their ghostly expressions strike us
as equally. And scary.
The gist of it being:

    Their morning our eventual afternoon
    who's driven in mumbling something about rendezvous
    then larking in that sharp imperative tone.
    Raising the hackles of gravel and tufts.

    All of a sudden.

One can, of course, console oneself
and even evolve with the pestilent mob.

Sleeping.
As usual.

Likewise

I am muted by a command that pervades
solitary in the apparently structureless.
Strange things to say.

Like it isn't and you don't
having less as more or
less is more or

if you come to think of it – a single number –
as strange, bear in mind lots and
lots and lots of them.

Then stand clear.
Grant them passage to the only place
in the world that matters

where new-found or -fangled strength enters
an isolated limb.
With foliage or with the hand.

Lads be limber, then in good sooth
vouch for the proffered image
whose glossaries still list.

Tell us what happens with the resolution
when all of them spring to mind.
Like surprises, only a lot more surprised.

Then let's decide where the mirror should go.
In it everything looks pretty much the same.
Which puzzles me still.

Solace

                    Say, rather
the tiny embodiment compressed
into a sudden space.
A miraculous return to nature.
Faces of saints

flushed slightly when we
falter
we peers and siblings.

No sweat.
No distinguishing scars.
Only your imagination
or mine.

Its glacial facial features
very quiet
and very, very
still.

Interval

But then but then who thought to choose
between the fact of dried blooms
and their delivery

between gravity and its source
of endless fascination
now coated with melted wax.

Yet no set pattern emerges
through anything that flows
save the white in this particular grove

interrupted
by three rob   rob   robins
on the lawn below

and the disquieting quiet of a jackrabbit
pensive
as tall as
a house.

Now these two terms
have to have
a counterpoise to keep

sinews to shuffle or bend
an insignificant remark
into something of a legend.

Not despite
but
because of.

And somewhere in there
between winter and our dismay
there is really a question

wending its way beyond the dead end
its features magnified
by the candle it carries.

It by itself.
Bit by bit.
Both like and utterly unlike.

The Final Analysis

A misnomer applied
to a single frequency
behaves much like

            and magnetism ranging
readily as far as
the channels.

Never the

nevertheless
the very notion among them.

A loud
and persistent
hum.

Full Disclosure

How best to combine the entries
from a dictionary so hotly contested
with a slim book bearing a thousand precautions
manifest in limpid tones.

For this or that to translate from whisper to thunder
and back again
whilst across the grassy levels
full measures of certainty drift.

At every juncture the focus shifts
to a soundpost crawling out from under
a hermetic glass bell.

Heretofore: Vexation.
Hereafter: Translucent.   Golden.   Depths.

Life Spans

Curved space.
A frothing.
An infancy of unmistakable
traces.

The sphere extrapolates
by extrapolation
(then)
its own pale shadow.

Behind the curve
or beyond it.

The intermediary
– which *is* which –
swirls within
a system

an impeccable rhythm
of intricate intricate trains

begging to be signaled out
where
one of an infinite number
of twins wonders:

> How fast
> and
> in what direction?

Whose timing in turn
depends on
how it came to be

by the by the
by the by.

Apparently
out of nothing.

Then the tiniest departure.

And so on.

Additional Reading

(1)

Preconceptions of landscape differ from their surroundings
displaying none of the periodic droughts
the shallow stretches
failing to shimmer between hence and forward.
By exposure to inhibition they have learned
to detach and brood
supervising a merciless hunger kept in clefts.

I think a relatively long span has something to do
with this.
(Capturing the imagination I mean.)

★

Be watchful and likely a twist could stir
the prospect of varied terrain
of dogs or ducks or the ability to see
the rare exception from a multiple perspective.
Everything present, albeit turning at different speeds.

★

A dreamer executes its likeness through cause
and effects an emphasis on sight in the midst of
voices from the *inside* which say: wet stones.
The smell of cut grass and low-lying boulders
effectively moves them then beyond *some* kind of threshold.

(2)

When the page of a huge white book says
do not elaborate
well then

                                  *

A young astronomer is well advised to
suspend the forgeries when contours are lacking
and position the sky for us all to observe 'empty'.
Reliable sources argue that this approach would
facilitate any number of happy outcomes.
In the meantime, a closet, a kitchen, a kitchen closet
offer a running commentary on something personal
brought forth in the presence of slightly worn hollows.

                                  *

Let the reader note:
> There are no guarantees in the search for authenticity
> only charred bone fragments pocketed by a stretch
> of clarity.

(3)

Village or pillage, our understanding of narrative suffers
the familiar fate of abandoned cabins.
From folding chairs to chopping trees, the means
to negotiate recovery – even in tiny instalments –
necessitates a remarkable lure.
An early column in this series attracted one curious item
with an impression that resembled
       if not the narrow ends of a plot
       then a measureless embrace that spoke of intricate
ardour
       I mean order.
No one treated this more eloquently than
the interlocking plates of some turtle shells
which illustrated simple, numerical regularity.

                          ★

It is the clam's claim to fame that its valves advance
a central paradox in any emergent pattern.
We are derailed (analogically) if we take this for
any old garden-variety snail.

                          ★

The former epitome.
The latter accessible only on foot.

(4)

In the absence of an editor, neither cite nor
cipher nor a bandeau of tightly flowered material
could unlace these unearthly and somewhat triangular
expressions.
They had come to seem.

★

Whether ye be a medieval doctor or some cellular substance
ingested accidentally into the field of ethnobotanical
research, consider
the relationship of three separate references.

Are they flowering?
Is there illness or evidence of unnatural whiteness
that may or may not include an errant iceberg
and its effects on the body?

★

Arranged alphabetically and laid out in sequence
there is always a risk of inversion.
Chapter Eleven is comprehensive on this subject.

(5)

Nevertheless survives the adage
to spell or bind
but tenderly
denotes the mark of passionate and tangled relics.
This could be intentional
or
this could be the pivoting.

*

For something in composition has set to work.
                    the midst of
still the case.

*

We require no evidence for the advent of a small leaf
or chapter
to read how or dwell in.
Just light swells.

(6)

Perhaps one should try to ignore lampposts
and instead divert incoherent
mutterings or
perhaps a watershed inclines the floating object to shift
ever
so slightly.
No meaning or moral implied.

                              ★

We have witnessed the means of seeing a valuable likeness
happier in a foreign home
and have dared to suggest (oh solicitor of speech)
that sultry summer mornings inhabit
apparitions of boats and maps and all those things
that drift.
But how to tell.

                              ★

Between you and me and the lamppost
there lies an inability to keep a secret.
On this the go-between depends.

'… where I'm at, and how to get out of being at here.'

— *Bugs Bunny*

Notes

'With Rumi' incorporates several phrases of '1826' from Coleman Barks's collection of Rumi's poems, *Like This*.

'Advances' contains the quote 'passing strange' from Shakespeare's *Othello*, Act i, Scene iii.

'Before and After' contains the quote 'Pray meditate upon its poetry' from Pearl S. Buck's *Imperial Woman*.

★

Some of these pieces were previously published in *The Gig* (6) and in *Queen Street Quarterly* (1.3). 'The Shadow of Your Simile' was printed as a broadside by *sinovertan*.

Special thanks to Darren Wershler-Henry for bringing the book to press, to Alana Wilcox for guiding it through, and to Rick/Simon for his visual translation. Thanks also to the Ontario Arts Council for its financial assistance.

About the Author

Lise Downe is the author of two previous books of poetry, *A Velvet Increase of Curiosity* and *The Soft Signature*. Originally from London, Ontario, she resides in Toronto where she also practices goldsmithing.

Typeset in Dante and Syndor
Printed and bound at the Coach House on bpNichol Lane, 2002

Edited and designed by Darren Wershler-Henry
Copy edited by Alana Wilcox
Cover design by Rick/Simon

Read the online version of this text at our website:
www.chbooks.com

Send us a request to be added to our mailing list:
mail@chbooks.com

Call us toll-free:
1 800 367 6360

Coach House Books
401 Huron Street (rear) on bpNichol Lane
Toronto, Ontario
M5S 2G5